Conquered

And

Rise!

Preface:

This book is a poetry book which has 26 pages written in English □ the book is about uplifting and healing the broken soul and keep them motivated and fueled.

With a great pleasure. For sure I know that poetic world is the most funny and enjoyable one. It is with my excitement to make it clear to you that there is no way that you would remain the same after reading the poems in this book.

"Only the very few weak-minded refuse to be influenced by literature and poetry"

<u>*One day*</u>

One day my mind, soul, blood,

Bone will need to rest .one day I

Will need my time alone .to clear my

Mind. I will need to go away on a

Vacation .one day I will have to go.

One day after my struggle I will need

Peace of mind .where I will be left alone

.at a peaceful days where nobody will be

Will disturb me.one day I will smile for

The last time.one day.

By takalani p

Why woman?

What happen to woman .what have?

They done to deserve so much hatreds.

Why must she receive a flower on her?

Last day on earth. What has become of

Us as man. Why woman

You made a vow and said "until death do

Us apart while you are the one who want

To do it apart. If they don't feel safe around

Us where they going to feel safe. Heaven. Where

On earth they gonna feel love and appreciated.

Slaughtering and beetling our mother is that the

Authority of man being the head of the family

When you look into her eyes and say you love her

What do you mean? How can you hurt someone?

That you love why you don't spread love as much

As you spread hate towards woman .why woman

Who is gonna protect our mother, sisters if
    people

Who were supposed to protect them has
    transmute to

Be devil . Monster seeking for a blood. Do that

To make her Happy when they die begging for
    their life. Die in

The Struggle of firhgting.is that the love, care,
    respect

You promise to give her. Why woman?

By takalani p

After

After all my effort allow me to go

And take a walk. A break to clear my

Mind .after all my struggle let me take

A deep breath. After all my hard work

Allow me to chase my dream after all the

Mountains I have climbed .after allow me to

Travel the world visit all the place I dreamed

Of and after all let me rest in peace. After

BY TAKALANI P

<u>WHEN AM CRYING</u>

Am not crying because am hurt

 Not because my heart is broken

I'm not even disappointed

I am crying to express how jubilant I am

In words I can't

But this is tears of joy. Am over wrath and

Respite. When I cry.

BY TAKALANI P

<u>My love</u>

Your beautiful face I scared.

 I hate you when you talk to me

Because you make me run out of words.

 You make me sing and dance a tune of
    your love

I know it's only yesterday

I need you, us, my love

Every time when I touch you

When I talk to YOU

Whenever I see you when I think for you

I feel love deep natural love

When you are FAR AWAY

I feel like you are gone forever

WHEN you say goodbye

I feel like I will never see your face

Again

I didn't know that you are the treasure am
     looking FOR

I don't know that you are the half of my
     heart

And with you my world is complete

And I want to CRAWL

Walk, jog, jump, run and fly with

 You in the name of love

My love for you is eternal

BY TAKALANI P

Love always leave a mark

I search for love in many place and people

I saw beautiful face and pretty girls

But my heart chose you

Among billions people

The love you gave and show you is
    undefined

And made to fulfil my wish to love .you
    made my heart itching to give my love

You truly create miracle, it was a dream
    come true

You are a soul mate, you believe in me
    when nobody else do

You know me better than I know myself
you made face

My deepest fear. You made my heart be
    where it should be

In a comfort zone, you made it easy for
me to love

You transmute into a monster you broke
and destroy what we built together

I thought it will never end

The wounds and pain, the scratch in my
heart

You made irremovable mark this hole you
create nobody will never be

Occupied and heal love always leave a
mark.

BY TAKALANI P

Mommy's pain

I watch you struggling crawling like a baby

Try to make a living but still you pretend
    to be strong

But I know deep down you broken .you

Were bleeding.at your eyes you cry tears
    but deep down you are crying blood?

She keep hustling trying to put food on
table

Sometimes she boil water until we sleep

Sometimes you cry but tears are no longer
    running because your eyes were so red

She even do things that I never thought

You could do mommy's pain

She turn to be a laughing stock

But she never care

Mommy's pain she taught me that "never
    be ashamed of your hustles

Better to be dirty to get food than to clean

And hungry because no one else will feed
you when are hungry

Mommy's pain to you strong women?

BY TAKALANI P

When am on my way

When am on my way don't say goodbye

Because am still coming back.

Don't miss me, I will give you a call

When am on my way sing the song I love?

pray for me to go well and I will pray too

Hold on… I am on my way!

When am on my way I will be happy

Because you and I we knew each other

We had a good time you

You gave me a good, greet memories

Memory that give me courage

I will tell others how you and I we used to
    laugh.

And playing, loving, and taking care of
    each other

But hold on am on my way!

BY TAKALANI P

<u>*I thought*</u>

I thought I am the master of it all

I thought I don't need anyone

I thought I can but the truth is I can't

I thought I have everything I want

I thought I don't care about anyone

I thought I got it all

I thought I don't LOVE YOU

But I do feel the love when you TALK

I feel natural love, I do feel CHEMISTRY

I feel your presence IN your ABSENCE

I thought I don't need anyone

But the truth is I need not anyone but you

BY TAKALANI P

<u>Dying sad</u>

I try to go and look for you

I was crying out loud for your
        FORGIVENESS

    I called, I texted... Several times

But I didn't get respond from you

Kept on hoping that one day, one day!

I will hear from you.

All I want was to reconcile with you

MAKING peace with you

And let bygone be the bygone.

Now my time is running out

I no longer have STRENGTH

My day has finally come

And I hope THIS letter get to you on time

By TAKALANI P

Sometimes I feel like am living my life in a
  Cage

 I feel so small and I can't even

fly, run nor jump.

 I feel like there is nobody in this world

 I feel lost and loneliness.

Sometimes I feel like I need fresh start

I feel like I need some strange people

People who don't know me

Even though running AWAY

Has never been a solution

But sometimes I just wanna go away

 far from here.

Sometimes I want somebody to love,

care, and be there for me.

I just want a shoulder to cry on

I want someone who won't give up on me

  Someone I can be of proud

I can proudly say "those are my siblings"

I want to love, to be loved is that much to
    ask for?

BY TAKALANI P

When I am alone

Don't read my mind because you won't get

anything

 When you try, you will go with it all

Wrong!

When am alone I am not sad, not angry

I just want my own time…

My I time!

Peace of moment to think trough.

By takalani p

My memory box

Whenever I miss you

 I just open my memory box

When I feel lonely Still my memory box

It make me feel alive and feel next to you.

I can feel your present in my memory box

I have stored a good memory that remind
    me of you

How sweet and kind you are

 All those sweet memory…

Sweet memories remind me how much I

Have fallen, fallen in a hard-memorable

Those were the days inside my

memory box !

By takalani p

Takalani Phathutshedzo was born in 16 July 1998, raised in Limpopo, and completed his matric. To further his studies he went to Tshisimani College, studying electrical engineering. Although, around mid-year he drop out and decided to follow his dream to be an author. According to him, he said "I believe in creating my own destination and now am full and dedicated myself in writing as a way of inspiring the world by the words in writing books"

"I believe in creating my own
destination and now am full and
dedicated myself in writing as a
way of inspiring the world by
the words in writing books"

Takalani p.

"Whenever I miss you

I just open my memory box"

"Don't read my mind because you won't
get anything"

"Sometimes I feel like I need fresh start

I feel like I need some strange people"

"Even though running AWAY

Has never been a solution"

ABOUT CHANGE PUBLICATION:

Change Publication, is an independent publishing brand. Founded by Phumudzo Mudau. It was established in 30 March 2020. Its responsibility is to take aspects of all the books published with us. Whereas, our aim is to attract good authors and publish books that achieve commercial success. We carry all aspects of publication: work to editors, designers and marketing specialists. We understand that, many authors' especially beginners tend to struggle financially, grammatically. But that is where we gets in; helping the disadvantaged, rejected authors by big brands and bring their books to life. However, distance can never be a barrier. Just one phone call or email can turn your life around. As a growing brand with international record of publication, one must never think "miss" to be part of such world-class establishment. We do not care about your money, we care

about making your book and seeing it
selling.

www.ingramcontent.com/pod-product-compliance
Lightning Source LLC
Chambersburg PA
CBHW071301130726
47998CB00003B/1281